FOREWORD

The collection of "Everything Will Be Okay" travel phrasebooks published by T&P Books is designed for people traveling abroad for tourism and business. The phrasebooks contain what matters most - the essentials for basic communication. This is an indispensable set of phrases to "survive" while abroad.

This phrasebook will help you in most cases where you need to ask something, get directions, find out how much something costs, etc. It can also resolve difficult communication situations where gestures just won't help.

This book contains a lot of phrases that have been grouped according to the most relevant topics. You'll also find a mini dictionary with useful words - numbers, time, calendar, colors...

Take "Everything Will Be Okay" phrasebook with you on the road and you'll have an irreplaceable traveling companion who will help you find your way out of any situation and teach you to not fear speaking with foreigners.

TABLE OF CONTENTS

T&P Books Publishing

Travel phrasebooks collection
«Everything Will Be Okay!»

T&P Books Publishing

PHRASEBOOK
INDONESIAN

THE MOST IMPORTANT PHRASES

This phrasebook contains
the most important
phrases and questions
for basic communication
Everything you need
to survive overseas

T&P BOOKS

By Andrey Taranov

Phrasebook + 250-word dictionary

English-Indonesian phrasebook & mini dictionary

By Andrey Taranov

The collection of "Everything Will Be Okay" travel phrasebooks published by T&P Books is designed for people traveling abroad for tourism and business. The phrasebooks contain what matters most - the essentials for basic communication. This is an indispensable set of phrases to "survive" while abroad.

You'll also find a mini dictionary with 250 useful words required for everyday communication - the names of months and days of the week, measurements, family members, and more.

T&P Books Publishing
www.tpbooks.com

ISBN: 978-1-80001-571-5

This book is also available in E-book formats.
Please visit www.tpbooks.com or the major online bookstores.

PRONUNCIATION

Letter	Indonesian example	T&P phonetic alphabet	English example
Aa	zaman	[a]	shorter than in ask
Bb	besar	[b]	baby, book
Cc	kecil, cepat	[tʃ]	church, French
Dd	dugaan	[d]	day, doctor
Ee	segera, mencium	[e], [ə]	medal, elm
Ff	berfungsi	[f]	face, food
Gg	juga, lagi	[g]	game, gold
Hh	hanya, bahwa	[h]	home, have
Ii	izin, sebagai ganti	[i], [j]	Peter, yard
Jj	setuju, ijin	[dʒ]	jeans, gin
Kk	kemudian, tidak	[k], [']	kiss, glottal stop
Ll	dilarang	[l]	lace, people
Mm	melihat	[m]	magic, milk
Nn	berenang	[n], [ŋ]	name, ring
Oo	toko roti	[oː]	fall, bomb
Pp	peribahasa	[p]	pencil, private
Qq	Aquarius	[k]	clock, kiss
Rr	ratu, riang	[r]	trilled [r]
Ss	sendok, syarat	[s], [ʃ]	city, machine
Tt	tamu, adat	[t]	tourist, trip
Uu	ambulans	[u]	book
Vv	renovasi	[v]	very, river
Ww	pariwisata	[w]	vase, winter
Xx	boxer	[ks]	box, taxi
Yy	banyak, syarat	[j]	yes, New York
Zz	zamrud	[z]	zebra, please

Combinations of letters

aa	maaf	[aʔa]	a+glottal stop
kh	khawatir	[h]	home, have
th	Gereja Lutheran	[t]	tourist, trip
-k	tidak	[']	glottal stop

LIST OF ABBREVIATIONS

English abbreviations

ab.	-	about
adj	-	adjective
adv	-	adverb
anim.	-	animate
as adj	-	attributive noun used as adjective
e.g.	-	for example
etc.	-	et cetera
fam.	-	familiar
fem.	-	feminine
form.	-	formal
inanim.	-	inanimate
masc.	-	masculine
math	-	mathematics
mil.	-	military
n	-	noun
pl	-	plural
pron.	-	pronoun
sb	-	somebody
sing.	-	singular
sth	-	something
v aux	-	auxiliary verb
vi	-	intransitive verb
vi, vt	-	intransitive, transitive verb
vt	-	transitive verb

T&P BOOKS

INDONESIAN PHRASEBOOK

This section contains important phrases that may come in handy in various real-life situations.
The phrasebook will help you ask for directions, clarify a price, buy tickets, and order food at a restaurant

T&P Books Publishing

PHRASEBOOK
CONTENTS

T&P Books Publishing

The bare minimum

Excuse me, ...	**Permisi, ...** [permisi, ...]
Hello.	**Halo.** [halo]
Thank you.	**Terima kasih.** [terima kasih]
Good bye.	**Selamat tinggal.** [slamat tiŋgal]
Yes.	**Ya.** [ja]
No.	**Tidak.** [tida']
I don't know.	**Saya tidak tahu.** [saja tida' tahu]
Where? | Where to? | When?	**Di mana? | Ke mana? | Kapan?** [di mana? | ke mana? | kapan?]

I need ...	**Saya perlu ...** [saja perlu ...]
I want ...	**Saya ingin ...** [saja iŋin ...]
Do you have ...?	**Apa Anda punya ...?** [apa anda punja ...?]
Is there a ... here?	**Apa ada ... di sini?** [apa ada ... di sini?]
May I ...?	**Boleh saya ...?** [boleh saja ...?]
..., please (polite request)	**Tolong, ...** [toloŋ, ...]

I'm looking for ...	**Saya sedang mencari ...** [saja sedaŋ mentʃari ...]
the restroom	**kamar kecil** [kamar ketʃil]
an ATM	**ATM** [a-te-em]
a pharmacy (drugstore)	**apotek** [apote']
a hospital	**rumah sakit** [rumah sakit]
the police station	**kantor polisi** [kantor polisi]
the subway	**stasiun bawah tanah** [stasiun bawah tanah]

a taxi **taksi**
[taksi]

the train station **stasiun kereta api**
[stasiun kereta api]

My name is … **Nama saya ...**
[nama saja ...]

What's your name? **Siapa nama Anda?**
[siapa nama anda?]

Could you please help me? **Bisakah Anda menolong saya?**
[bisakah anda menoloŋ saja?]

I've got a problem. **Saya sedang kesulitan.**
[saja sedaŋ kesulitan]

I don't feel well. **Saya tidak enak badan.**
[saja tida' enak badan]

Call an ambulance! **Panggil ambulans!**
[paŋgil ambulans!]

May I make a call? **Boleh saya menelepon?**
[boleh saja menelepon?]

I'm sorry. **Maaf.**
[ma'af]

You're welcome. **Terima kasih kembali.**
[terima kasih kembali]

I, me **Saya, aku**
[saja, aku]

you (inform.) **kamu, kau**
[kamu, kau]

he **dia, ia**
[dia, ia]

she **dia, ia**
[dia, ia]

they (masc.) **mereka**
[mereka]

they (fem.) **mereka**
[mereka]

we **kami**
[kami]

you (pl) **kalian**
[kalian]

you (sg, form.) **Anda**
[anda]

ENTRANCE **MASUK**
[masu']

EXIT **KELUAR**
[keluar]

OUT OF ORDER **TIDAK DAPAT DIGUNAKAN**
[tida' dapat digunakan]

CLOSED **TUTUP**
[tutup]

OPEN	**BUKA** [buka]
FOR WOMEN	**UNTUK PEREMPUAN** [untu' perempuan]
FOR MEN	**UNTUK LAKI-LAKI** [untu' laki-laki]

Questions

Where?	**Di mana?** [di mana?]
Where to?	**Ke mana?** [ke mana?]
Where from?	**Dari mana?** [dari mana?]
Why?	**Kenapa?** [kenapa?]
For what reason?	**Untuk apa?** [untu' apa?]
When?	**Kapan?** [kapan?]
How long?	**Berapa lama?** [berapa lama?]
At what time?	**Jam berapa?** [dʒam berapa?]
How much?	**Berapa harganya?** [berapa harganja?]
Do you have ...?	**Apa Anda punya ...?** [apa anda punja ...?]
Where is ...?	**Di mana ...?** [di mana ...?]
What time is it?	**Jam berapa sekarang?** [dʒam berapa sekaraŋ?]
May I make a call?	**Boleh saya menelepon?** [boleh saja menelepon?]
Who's there?	**Siapa di sana?** [siapa di sana?]
Can I smoke here?	**Boleh saya merokok di sini?** [boleh saja meroko' di sini?]
May I ...?	**Boleh saya ...?** [boleh saja ...?]

Needs

I'd like …	**Saya hendak ...** [saja henda' ...]
I don't want …	**Saya tidak ingin ...** [saja tida' iŋin ...]
I'm thirsty.	**Saya haus.** [saja haus]
I want to sleep.	**Saya ingin tidur.** [saja iŋin tidur]
I want …	**Saya ingin ...** [saja iŋin ...]
to wash up	**mandi** [mandi]
to brush my teeth	**menyikat gigi** [menjikat gigi]
to rest a while	**istirahat sebentar** [istirahat sebentar]
to change my clothes	**ganti pakaian** [ganti pakajan]
to go back to the hotel	**kembali ke hotel** [kembali ke hotel]
to buy …	**membeli ...** [membeli ...]
to go to …	**pergi ke ...** [pergi ke ...]
to visit …	**mengunjungi ...** [meŋundʒ'uŋi ...]
to meet with …	**bertemu dengan ...** [bertemu deŋan ...]
to make a call	**menelepon** [menelepon]
I'm tired.	**Saya lelah.** [saja lelah]
We are tired.	**Kami lelah.** [kami lelah]
I'm cold.	**Saya kedinginan.** [saja kediŋinan]
I'm hot.	**Saya kepanasan.** [saja kepanasan]
I'm OK.	**Saya baik-baik saja.** [saja bai'-bai' sadʒ'a]

I need to make a call.

Saya perlu menelepon.
[saja perlu menelepon]

I need to go to the restroom.

Saya perlu pergi ke kamar kecil.
[saja perlu pergi ke kamar ketʃil]

I have to go.

Saya harus pergi.
[saja harus pergi]

I have to go now.

Saya harus pergi sekarang.
[saja harus pergi sekaraŋ]

Asking for directions

Excuse me, ...	**Permisi, ...** [permisi, ...]
Where is ...?	**Di mana ...?** [di mana ...?]
Which way is ...?	**Ke manakah arah ke ...?** [ke manakah arah ke ...?]
Could you help me, please?	**Bisakah Anda menolong saya?** [bisakah anda menoloŋ saja?]
I'm looking for ...	**Saya sedang mencari ...** [saja sedaŋ mentʃari ...]
I'm looking for the exit.	**Saya sedang mencari pintu keluar.** [saja sedaŋ mentʃari pintu keluar]
I'm going to ...	**Saya akan pergi ke ...** [saja akan pergi ke ...]
Am I going the right way to ...?	**Benarkah ini jalan ke ...?** [benarkah ini dʒˈalan ke ...?]
Is it far?	**Apakah tempatnya jauh?** [apakah tempatnja dʒˈauh?]
Can I get there on foot?	**Bisakah saya berjalan kaki ke sana?** [bisakah saja berdʒˈalan kaki ke sana?]
Can you show me on the map?	**Bisakah Anda tunjukkan di peta?** [bisakah anda tundʒˈuʔkan di peta?]
Show me where we are right now.	**Tunjukkan di mana lokasi kita sekarang.** [tundʒˈuʔkan di mana lokasi kita sekaraŋ]
Here	**Di sini** [di sini]
There	**Di sana** [di sana]
This way	**Jalan ini** [dʒˈalan ini]
Turn right.	**Belok kanan.** [belo' kanan]
Turn left.	**Belok kiri.** [belo' kiri]
first (second, third) turn	**belokan pertama (kedua, ketiga)** [belokan pertama (kedua, ketiga)]
to the right	**ke kanan** [ke kanan]

to the left	**ke kiri** [ke kiri]
Go straight ahead.	**Lurus terus.** [lurus terus]

Signs

WELCOME!	**SELAMAT DATANG!** [selamat dataŋ!]
ENTRANCE	**MASUK** [masuʔ]
EXIT	**KELUAR** [keluar]
PUSH	**DORONG** [doroŋ]
PULL	**TARIK** [tariʔ]
OPEN	**BUKA** [buka]
CLOSED	**TUTUP** [tutup]
FOR WOMEN	**UNTUK PEREMPUAN** [untuʔ perempuan]
FOR MEN	**UNTUK LAKI-LAKI** [untuʔ laki-laki]
GENTLEMEN, GENTS	**PRIA** [pria]
WOMEN	**WANITA** [wanita]
DISCOUNTS	**DISKON** [diskon]
SALE	**OBRAL** [obral]
FREE	**GRATIS** [gratis]
NEW!	**BARU!** [baru!]
ATTENTION!	**PERHATIAN!** [perhatian!]
NO VACANCIES	**KAMAR PENUH** [kamar penuh]
RESERVED	**DIPESAN** [dipesan]
ADMINISTRATION	**ADMINISTRASI** [administrasi]
STAFF ONLY	**HANYA UNTUK STAF** [hanja untuʔ staf]

BEWARE OF THE DOG! **AWAS ANJING GALAK!**
[awas andʒiŋ galaʔ!]

NO SMOKING! **DILARANG MEROKOK!**
[dilaraŋ merokoʔ!]

DO NOT TOUCH! **JANGAN SENTUH!**
[dʒʲaŋan sentuh!]

DANGEROUS **BERBAHAYA**
[berbahaja]

DANGER **BAHAYA**
[bahaja]

HIGH VOLTAGE **TEGANGAN TINGGI**
[tegaŋan tiŋgi]

NO SWIMMING! **DILARANG BERENANG!**
[dilaraŋ berenaŋ!]

OUT OF ORDER **TIDAK DAPAT DIGUNAKAN**
[tidaʔ dapat digunakan]

FLAMMABLE **MUDAH TERBAKAR**
[mudah terbakar]

FORBIDDEN **DILARANG**
[dilaraŋ]

NO TRESPASSING! **DILARANG MASUK!**
[dilaraŋ masuʔ!]

WET PAINT **CAT BASAH**
[tʃat basah]

CLOSED FOR RENOVATIONS **DITUTUP KARENA ADA PERBAIKAN**
[ditutup karena ada perbaikan]

WORKS AHEAD **ADA PROYEK DI DEPAN**
[ada projeʔ di depan]

DETOUR **JALUR ALTERNATIF**
[dʒʲalur alternatif]

Transportation. General phrases

plane	**pesawat** [pesawat]
train	**kereta api** [kereta api]
bus	**bus** [bus]
ferry	**feri** [feri]
taxi	**taksi** [taksi]
car	**mobil** [mobil]

schedule	**jadwal** [dʒadwal]
Where can I see the schedule?	**Di mana saya dapat melihat jadwalnya?** [di mana saja dapat melihat dʒadwalnja?]
workdays (weekdays)	**hari kerja** [hari kerdʒa]
weekends	**akhir pekan** [ahir pekan]
holidays	**hari libur** [hari libur]

DEPARTURE	**KEBERANGKATAN** [keberaŋkatan]
ARRIVAL	**KEDATANGAN** [kedataŋan]
DELAYED	**DITUNDA** [ditunda]
CANCELLED	**DIBATALKAN** [dibatalkan]

next (train, etc.)	**berikutnya** [berikutnja]
first	**pertama** [pertama]
last	**terakhir** [terahir]

When is the next ...?	**Kapan ... berikutnya?** [kapan ... berikutnja?]
When is the first ...?	**Kapan ... pertama?** [kapan ... pertama?]
When is the last ...?	**Kapan ... terakhir?** [kapan ... terahir?]

transfer (change of trains, etc.)	**pindah** [pindah]
to make a transfer	**berpindah** [berpindah]
Do I need to make a transfer?	**Haruskah saya berpindah?** [haruskah saja berpindah?]

Buying tickets

Where can I buy tickets?	**Di mana saya dapat membeli tiket?** [di mana saja dapat membeli tiket?]
ticket	**tiket** [tiket]
to buy a ticket	**membeli tiket** [membeli tiket]
ticket price	**harga tiket** [harga tiket]
Where to?	**Ke mana?** [ke mana?]
To what station?	**Ke stasiun apa?** [ke stasiun apa?]
I need ...	**Saya perlu ...** [saja perlu ...]
one ticket	**satu tiket** [satu tiket]
two tickets	**dua tiket** [dua tiket]
three tickets	**tiga tiket** [tiga tiket]
one-way	**sekali jalan** [sekali dʒ'alan]
round-trip	**pulang pergi** [pulaŋ pergi]
first class	**kelas satu** [kelas satu]
second class	**kelas dua** [kelas dua]
today	**hari ini** [hari ini]
tomorrow	**besok** [beso']
the day after tomorrow	**lusa** [lusa]
in the morning	**pagi** [pagi]
in the afternoon	**siang** [siaŋ]
in the evening	**malam** [malam]

aisle seat

kursi dekat lorong
[kursi dekat loroŋ]

window seat

kursi dekat jendela
[kursi dekat ʤˈendela]

How much?

Berapa harganya?
[berapa harganja?]

Can I pay by credit card?

Bisakah saya membayar dengan kartu kredit?
[bisakah saja membajar deŋan kartu kredit?]

Bus

bus	**bus** [bus]
intercity bus	**bus antarkota** [bus antarkota]
bus stop	**pemberhentian bus** [pemberhentian bus]
Where's the nearest bus stop?	**Di mana pemberhentian bus terdekat?** [di mana pemberhentian bus terdekat?]
number (bus ~, etc.)	**nomor** [nomor]
Which bus do I take to get to ...?	**Bus apa yang ke ...?** [bus apa jaŋ ke ...?]
Does this bus go to ...?	**Apakah bus ini ke ...?** [apakah bus ini ke ...?]
How frequent are the buses?	**Seberapa sering busnya datang?** [seberapa seriŋ busnja dataŋ?]
every 15 minutes	**setiap 15 menit** [setiap lima belas menit]
every half hour	**setiap setengah jam** [setiap seteŋah dʒʲam]
every hour	**setiap jam** [setiap dʒʲam]
several times a day	**beberapa kali sehari** [beberapa kali sehari]
... times a day	**... kali sehari** [... kali sehari]
schedule	**jadwal** [dʒʲadwal]
Where can I see the schedule?	**Di mana saya dapat melihat jadwalnya?** [di mana saja dapat melihat dʒʲadwalnja?]
When is the next bus?	**Kapan bus berikutnya?** [kapan bus berikutnja?]
When is the first bus?	**Kapan bus pertama?** [kapan bus pertama?]
When is the last bus?	**Kapan bus terakhir?** [kapan bus terahir?]

stop

pemberhentian
[pemberhentian]

next stop

pemberhentian berikutnya
[pemberhentian berikutnja]

last stop (terminus)

pemberhentian terakhir (terminal)
[pemberhentian terahir (terminal)]

Stop here, please.

Berhenti di sini.
[berhenti di sini]

Excuse me, this is my stop.

Permisi, saya turun di sini.
[permisi, saja turun di sini]

Train

train	**kereta api** [kereta api]
suburban train	**kereta api lokal** [kereta api lokal]
long-distance train	**kereta api jarak jauh** [kereta api dʒˈarak dʒˈauh]
train station	**stasiun kereta api** [stasiun kereta api]
Excuse me, where is the exit to the platform?	**Permisi, di manakah pintu ke arah peron?** [permisi, di manakah pintu ke arah peron?]

Does this train go to …?	**Apakah kereta api ini menuju ke …?** [apakah kereta api ini menudʒˈu ke …?]
next train	**kereta api berikutnya** [kereta api berikutnja]
When is the next train?	**Kapan kereta api berikutnya?** [kapan kereta api berikutnja?]

Where can I see the schedule?	**Di mana saya dapat melihat jadwalnya?** [di mana saja dapat melihat dʒˈadwalnja?]
From which platform?	**Dari peron jalur berapa?** [dari peron dʒˈalur berapa?]
When does the train arrive in …?	**Kapan kereta api ini sampai di …?** [kapan kereta api ini sampaj di …?]

Please help me.	**Tolong bantu saya.** [toloŋ bantu saja]
I'm looking for my seat.	**Saya sedang mencari kursi saya.** [saja sedaŋ mentʃari kursi saja]
We're looking for our seats.	**Kami sedang mencari kursi kami.** [kami sedaŋ mentʃari kursi kami]

My seat is taken.	**Kursi saya sudah ditempati.** [kursi saja sudah ditempati]
Our seats are taken.	**Kursi kami sudah ditempati.** [kursi kami sudah ditempati]
I'm sorry but this is my seat.	**Maaf, ini kursi saya.** [maʔaf, ini kursi saja]

Is this seat taken?

Apakah kursi ini sudah diambil?
[apakah kursi ini sudah diambil?]

May I sit here?

Boleh saya duduk di sini?
[boleh saja dudu' di sini?]

On the train. Dialogue (No ticket)

Ticket, please.	**Permisi, tiketnya.** [permisi, tiketnja]
I don't have a ticket.	**Saya tidak punya tiket.** [saja tida' punja tiket]
I lost my ticket.	**Tiket saya hilang.** [tiket saja hilaŋ]
I forgot my ticket at home.	**Tiket saya tertinggal di rumah.** [tiket saja tertiŋgal di rumah]
You can buy a ticket from me.	**Anda bisa membeli tiket dari saya.** [anda bisa membeli tiket dari saja]
You will also have to pay a fine.	**Anda juga harus membayar denda.** [anda ʤuga harus membajar denda]
Okay.	**Baik.** [bai']
Where are you going?	**Ke manakah tujuan Anda?** [ke manakah tuʤuan anda?]
I'm going to …	**Saya akan pergi ke ...** [saja akan pergi ke ...]
How much? I don't understand.	**Berapa harganya? Saya tidak mengerti.** [berapa harganja? saja tida' meŋerti]
Write it down, please.	**Tolong tuliskan.** [toloŋ tuliskan]
Okay. Can I pay with a credit card?	**Baik. Bisakah saya membayar dengan kartu kredit?** [bai'. bisakah saja membajar deŋan kartu kredit?]
Yes, you can.	**Ya, bisa.** [ja, bisa]
Here's your receipt.	**Ini tanda terimanya.** [ini tanda terimanja]
Sorry about the fine.	**Maaf atas dendanya.** [ma'af atas dendanja]
That's okay. It was my fault.	**Tidak apa-apa. Saya yang salah.** [tida' apa-apa. saja jaŋ salah.]
Enjoy your trip.	**Selamat menikmati perjalanan.** [selamat menikmati perʤalanan]

Taxi

taxi
taksi
[taksi]

taxi driver
sopir taksi
[sopir taksi]

to catch a taxi
menyetop taksi
[menjetop taksi]

taxi stand
pangkalan taksi
[paŋkalan taksi]

Where can I get a taxi?
Di mana saya bisa mendapatkan taksi?
[di mana saja bisa mendapatkan taksi?]

to call a taxi
menelepon taksi
[menelepon taksi]

I need a taxi.
Saya perlu taksi.
[saja perlu taksi]

Right now.
Sekarang.
[sekaraŋ]

What is your address (location)?
Di mana alamat Anda?
[di mana alamat anda?]

My address is ...
Alamat saya di ...
[alamat saja di ...]

Your destination?
Tujuan Anda?
[tudʒ¡uan anda?]

Excuse me, ...
Permisi, ...
[permisi, ...]

Are you available?
Apa taksi ini kosong?
[apa taksi ini kosoŋ?]

How much is it to get to ...?
Berapa ongkos ke ...?
[berapa oŋkos ke ...?]

Do you know where it is?
Tahukah Anda tempatnya?
[tahukah anda tempatnja?]

Airport, please.
Ke bandara.
[ke bandara]

Stop here, please.
Berhenti di sini.
[berhenti di sini]

It's not here.
Bukan di sini.
[bukan di sini]

This is the wrong address.
Alamatnya salah.
[alamatnja salah]

Turn left.	**Belok kiri** [belo' kiri]
Turn right.	**Belok kanan.** [belo' kanan]

How much do I owe you?	**Berapa yang harus saya bayar?** [berapa jaŋ harus saja bajar?]
I'd like a receipt, please.	**Saya minta tanda terimanya.** [saja minta tanda terimanja]
Keep the change.	**Kembaliannya untuk Anda.** [kembaliannja untu' anda]

Would you please wait for me?	**Maukah Anda menunggu saya?** [maukah anda menuŋgu saja?]
five minutes	**lima menit** [lima menit]
ten minutes	**sepuluh menit** [sepuluh menit]
fifteen minutes	**lima belas menit** [lima belas menit]
twenty minutes	**dua puluh menit** [dua puluh menit]
half an hour	**setengah jam** [seteŋah dʒˈam]

Hotel

Hello.	**Halo.** [halo]
My name is …	**Nama saya ...** [nama saja ...]
I have a reservation.	**Saya sudah memesan.** [saja sudah memesan]
I need …	**Saya perlu ...** [saja perlu ...]
a single room	**kamar single** [kamar sinle]
a double room	**kamar double** [kamar double]
How much is that?	**Berapa harganya?** [berapa harganja?]
That's a bit expensive.	**Agak mahal.** [aga' mahal]
Do you have anything else?	**Apa Anda punya opsi lain?** [apa anda punja opsi lain?]
I'll take it.	**Saya ambil.** [saja ambil]
I'll pay in cash.	**Saya bayar tunai.** [saja bajar tunaj]
I've got a problem.	**Saya sedang kesulitan.** [saja sedaŋ kesulitan]
My … is broken.	**... saya rusak.** [... saja rusa']
My … is out of order.	**... saya tidak dapat digunakan.** [... saja tida' dapat digunakan]
TV	**TV** [tv]
air conditioner	**alat pendingin hawa** [alat pendiŋin hawa]
tap	**keran** [keran]
shower	**pancuran** [pantʃuran]
sink	**bak cuci** [ba' tʃutʃi]
safe	**brankas** [brankas]

door lock	**kunci pintu** [kuntʃi pintu]
electrical outlet	**stopkontak** [stopkontak]
hairdryer	**pegering rambut** [pegeriŋ rambut]

I don't have …	**Tidak ada …** [tida' ada …]
water	**air** [air]
light	**lampu** [lampu]
electricity	**listrik** [listri']

Can you give me …?	**Bisakah Anda memberi saya …?** [bisakah anda memberi saja …?]
a towel	**handuk** [handu']
a blanket	**selimut** [selimut]
slippers	**sandal** [sandal]
a robe	**jubah** [dʒubah]
shampoo	**sampo** [sampo]
soap	**sabun** [sabun]

I'd like to change rooms.	**Saya ingin pindah kamar.** [saja iŋin pindah kamar]
I can't find my key.	**Kunci saya tidak ketemu.** [kuntʃi saja tida' ketemu]
Could you open my room, please?	**Bisakah Anda membukakan pintu saya?** [bisakah anda membukakan pintu saja?]
Who's there?	**Siapa di sana?** [siapa di sana?]
Come in!	**Masuk!** [masu'!]
Just a minute!	**Tunggu sebentar!** [tuŋgu sebentar!]
Not right now, please.	**Jangan sekarang.** [dʒaŋan sekaraŋ]

Come to my room, please.	**Datanglah ke kamar saya.** [dataŋlah ke kamar saja]
I'd like to order food service.	**Saya ingin memesan makanan.** [saja iŋin memesan makanan]

My room number is …	**Nomor kamar saya …** [nomor kamar saja …]
I'm leaving …	**Saya pergi …** [saja pergi …]
We're leaving …	**Kami pergi …** [kami pergi …]
right now	**sekarang** [sekaraŋ]
this afternoon	**siang ini** [siaŋ ini]
tonight	**malam ini** [malam ini]
tomorrow	**besok** [beso']
tomorrow morning	**besok pagi** [beso' pagi]
tomorrow evening	**besok malam** [beso' malam]
the day after tomorrow	**lusa** [lusa]

I'd like to pay.	**Saya hendak membayar.** [saja henda' membajar]
Everything was wonderful.	**Segalanya luar biasa.** [segalanja luar biasa]
Where can I get a taxi?	**Di mana saya bisa mendapatkan taksi?** [di mana saja bisa mendapatkan taksi?]
Would you call a taxi for me, please?	**Bisakah Anda memanggilkan saya taksi?** [bisakah anda memaŋgilkan saja taksi?]

Restaurant

Can I look at the menu, please? **Bisakah saya melihat menunya?**
[bisakah saja melihat menunja?]

Table for one. **Meja untuk satu orang.**
[medʒa untu' satu oraŋ]

There are two (three, four) of us. **Kami berdua (bertiga, berempat).**
[kami berdua (bertiga, berempat)]

Smoking **Ruang Merokok**
[ruaŋ meroko']

No smoking **Ruang Bebas Rokok**
[ruaŋ bebas roko']

Excuse me! (addressing a waiter) **Permisi!**
[permisi!]

menu **menu**
[menu]

wine list **daftar anggur**
[daftar aŋgur]

The menu, please. **Tolong menunya.**
[toloŋ menunja]

Are you ready to order? **Apakah Anda siap memesan?**
[apakah anda siap memesan?]

What will you have? **Apa yang ingin Anda pesan?**
[apa jaŋ iŋin anda pesan?]

I'll have ... **Saya ingin memesan ...**
[saja iŋin memesan ...]

I'm a vegetarian. **Saya vegetarian.**
[saja vegetarian]

meat **daging**
[dagiŋ]

fish **ikan**
[ikan]

vegetables **sayur mayur**
[sajur majur]

Do you have vegetarian dishes? **Apa Anda punya hidangan vegetarian?**
[apa anda punja hidaŋan vegetarian?]

I don't eat pork. **Saya tidak makan daging babi.**
[saja tida' makan dagiŋ babi]

He /she/ doesn't eat meat. **Dia tidak makan daging.**
[dia tida' makan dagiŋ]

I am allergic to ... **Saya alergi ...**
[saja alergi ...]

Would you please bring me ...

Tolong ambilkan ...
[toloŋ ambilkan ...]

salt | pepper | sugar

garam | merica | gula
[garam | meritʃa | gula]

coffee | tea | dessert

kopi | teh | pencuci mulut
[kopi | teh | pentʃutʃi mulut]

water | sparkling | plain

air | air soda | air putih
[air | air soda | air putih]

a spoon | fork | knife

sendok | garpu | pisau
[sendo' | garpu | pisau]

a plate | napkin

piring | serbet
[piriŋ | serbet]

Enjoy your meal!

Selamat menikmati!
[selamat menikmati!]

One more, please.

Tambah satu lagi.
[tambah satu lagi]

It was very delicious.

Benar-benar lezat.
[benar-benar lezat]

check | change | tip

tagihan | kembalian | tip
[tagihan | kembalian | tip]

Check, please.
(Could I have the check, please?)

Tolong tagihannya.
[toloŋ tagihannja]

Can I pay by credit card?

Bisakah saya membayar dengan kartu kredit?
[bisakah saja membajar deŋan kartu kredit?]

I'm sorry, there's a mistake here.

Maaf, ada kesalahan di sini.
[ma'af, ada kesalahan di sini]

Shopping

Can I help you?	**Ada yang bisa saya bantu?** [ada jaŋ bisa saja bantu?]
Do you have …?	**Apa Anda punya …?** [apa anda punja …?]
I'm looking for …	**Saya sedang mencari …** [saja sedaŋ mentʃari …]
I need …	**Saya perlu …** [saja perlu …]
I'm just looking.	**Saya hanya melihat-lihat.** [saja hanja melihat-lihat]
We're just looking.	**Kami hanya melihat-lihat.** [kami hanja melihat-lihat]
I'll come back later.	**Saya akan kembali lagi nanti.** [saja akan kembali lagi nanti]
We'll come back later.	**Kami akan kembali lagi nanti.** [kami akan kembali lagi nanti]
discounts | sale	**diskon | obral** [diskon | obral]
Would you please show me …	**Bisakah Anda tunjukkan …** [bisakah anda tundʒuʔkan …]
Would you please give me …	**Bisakah Anda ambilkan …** [bisakah anda ambilkan …]
Can I try it on?	**Bisakah saya mencobanya?** [bisakah saja mentʃobanja?]
Excuse me, where's the fitting room?	**Permisi, di mana kamar pasnya?** [permisi, di mana kamar pasnja?]
Which color would you like?	**Warna apa yang Anda inginkan?** [warna apa jaŋ anda iŋinkan?]
size | length	**ukuran | panjang** [ukuran | pandʒiaŋ]
How does it fit?	**Apakah pas?** [apakah pas?]
How much is it?	**Berapa harganya?** [berapa harganja?]
That's too expensive.	**Itu terlalu mahal.** [itu terlalu mahal]
I'll take it.	**Saya ambil.** [saja ambil]
Excuse me, where do I pay?	**Permisi, di mana saya harus membayar?** [permisi, di mana saja harus membajar?]

Will you pay in cash or credit card? **Apakah Anda ingin membayar tunai atau dengan kartu kredit?**
[apakah anda iŋin membajar tunaj atau deŋan kartu kredit?]

In cash | with credit card **Tunai | dengan kartu kredit**
[tunaj | deŋan kartu kredit]

Do you want the receipt? **Apakah Anda ingin tanda terimanya?**
[apakah anda iŋin tanda terimanja?]

Yes, please. **Ya.**
[ja]

No, it's OK. **Tidak, tidak usah.**
[tidaʾ, tidaʾ usah]

Thank you. Have a nice day! **Terima kasih. Semoga hari Anda menyenangkan!**
[terima kasih. semoga hari anda menjenaŋkan!]

In town

Excuse me, …

Permisi, …
[permisi, …]

I'm looking for …

Saya sedang mencari ...
[saja sedaŋ mentʃari ...]

the subway

stasiun bawah tanah
[stasiun bawah tanah]

my hotel

hotel saya
[hotel saja]

the movie theater

bioskop
[bioskop]

a taxi stand

pangkalan taksi
[paŋkalan taksi]

an ATM

ATM
[a-te-em]

a foreign exchange office

tempat penukaran mata uang
[tempat penukaran mata uaŋ]

an internet café

warnet
[warnet]

… street

Jalan ...
[dʒʲalan ...]

this place

tempat ini
[tempat ini]

Do you know where … is?

Apakah Anda tahu lokasi ...?
[apakah anda tahu lokasi ...?]

Which street is this?

Jalan apakah ini?
[dʒʲalan apakah ini?]

Show me where we are right now.

**Tunjukkan di mana lokasi kita
sekarang.**
[tundʒʲuʔkan di mana lokasi kita
sekaraŋ]

Can I get there on foot?

Bisakah saya berjalan kaki ke sana?
[bisakah saja berdʒʲalan kaki ke sana?]

Do you have a map of the city?

Apa Anda punya peta kota?
[apa anda punja peta kota?]

How much is a ticket to get in?

Berapa harga tiket masuk?
[berapa harga tiket masuʔ?]

Can I take pictures here?

Bisakah saya berfoto di sini?
[bisakah saja berfoto di sini?]

Are you open?

Apakah Anda buka?
[apakah anda buka?]

When do you open?

Kapan Anda buka?
[kapan anda buka?]

When do you close?

Kapan Anda tutup?
[kapan anda tutup?]

Money

money	**uang** [uaŋ]
cash	**tunai** [tunaj]
paper money	**uang kertas** [uaŋ kertas]
loose change	**uang receh** [uaŋ retʃeh]
check | change | tip	**tagihan | kembalian | tip** [tagihan | kembalian | tip]
credit card	**kartu kredit** [kartu kredit]
wallet	**dompet** [dompet]
to buy	**membeli** [membeli]
to pay	**membayar** [membajar]
fine	**denda** [denda]
free	**gratis** [gratis]
Where can I buy ...?	**Di mana saya bisa membeli ...?** [di mana saja bisa membeli ...?]
Is the bank open now?	**Apakah bank buka sekarang?** [apakah ban' buka sekaraŋ?]
When does it open?	**Kapan bank buka?** [kapan bank buka?]
When does it close?	**Kapan bank tutup?** [kapan bank tutup?]
How much?	**Berapa harganya?** [berapa harganja?]
How much is this?	**Berapa harganya?** [berapa harganja?]
That's too expensive.	**Itu terlalu mahal.** [itu terlalu mahal]
Excuse me, where do I pay?	**Permisi, di mana saya harus membayar?** [permisi, di mana saja harus membajar?]

Check, please.

Tolong tagihannya.
[toloŋ tagihannja]

Can I pay by credit card?

Bisakah saya membayar dengan kartu kredit?
[bisakah saja membajar deŋan kartu kredit?]

Is there an ATM here?

Adakah ATM di sini?
[adakah a-te-em di sini?]

I'm looking for an ATM.

Saya sedang mencari ATM.
[saja sedaŋ menʧari a-te-em]

I'm looking for a foreign exchange office.

Saya sedang mencari tempat penukaran mata uang.
[saja sedaŋ menʧari tempat penukaran mata uaŋ]

I'd like to change …

Saya ingin menukarkan ...
[saja iŋin menukarkan ...]

What is the exchange rate?

Berapakah nilai tukarnya?
[berapakah nilaj tukarnja?]

Do you need my passport?

Apa Anda butuh paspor saya?
[apa anda butuh paspor saja?]

Time

What time is it?	**Jam berapa sekarang?** [dʒam berapa sekaraŋ?]
When?	**Kapan?** [kapan?]
At what time?	**Jam berapa?** [dʒam berapa?]
now | later | after …	**sekarang | nanti | setelah ...** [sekaraŋ | nanti | setelah ...]
one o'clock	**pukul satu** [pukul satu]
one fifteen	**pukul satu lewat lima belas** [pukul satu lewat lima belas]
one thirty	**pukul satu lewat tiga puluh** [pukul satu lewat tiga puluh]
one forty-five	**pukul satu lewat empat puluh lima** [pukul satu lewat empat puluh lima]
one | two | three	**satu | dua | tiga** [satu | dua | tiga]
four | five | six	**empat | lima | enam** [empat | lima | enam]
seven | eight | nine	**tujuh | delapan | sembilan** [tudʒuh | delapan | sembilan]
ten | eleven | twelve	**sepuluh | sebelas | dua belas** [sepuluh | sebelas | dua belas]
in …	**dalam ...** [dalam ...]
five minutes	**lima menit** [lima menit]
ten minutes	**sepuluh menit** [sepuluh menit]
fifteen minutes	**lima belas menit** [lima belas menit]
twenty minutes	**dua puluh menit** [dua puluh menit]
half an hour	**setengah jam** [seteŋah dʒam]
an hour	**satu jam** [satu dʒam]

in the morning	**pagi** [pagi]
early in the morning	**pagi-pagi sekali** [pagi-pagi sekali]
this morning	**pagi ini** [pagi ini]
tomorrow morning	**besok pagi** [beso' pagi]
in the middle of the day	**tengah hari** [teŋah hari]
in the afternoon	**siang** [siaŋ]
in the evening	**malam** [malam]
tonight	**malam ini** [malam ini]
at night	**pada malam hari** [pada malam hari]
yesterday	**kemarin** [kemarin]
today	**hari ini** [hari ini]
tomorrow	**besok** [beso']
the day after tomorrow	**lusa** [lusa]
What day is it today?	**Hari apa sekarang?** [hari apa sekaraŋ?]
It's …	**Sekarang ...** [sekaraŋ ...]
Monday	**Hari Senin** [hari senin]
Tuesday	**Hari Selasa** [hari selasa]
Wednesday	**Hari Rabu** [hari rabu]
Thursday	**Hari Kamis** [hari kamis]
Friday	**Hari Jumat** [hari dʒʲumat]
Saturday	**Hari Sabtu** [hari sabtu]
Sunday	**Hari Minggu** [hari miŋgu]

Greetings. Introductions

Hello.
Halo.
[halo]

Pleased to meet you.
Senang dapat berjumpa dengan Anda.
[senaŋ dapat berdʒ'umpa deŋan anda]

Me too.
Sama-sama.
[sama-sama]

I'd like you to meet …
Kenalkan, …
[kenalkan, …]

Nice to meet you.
Senang dapat berjumpa dengan Anda.
[senaŋ dapat berdʒ'umpa deŋan anda]

How are you?
Apa kabar?
[apa kabar?]

My name is …
Nama saya …
[nama saja …]

His name is …
Namanya …
[namanja …]

Her name is …
Namanya …
[namanja …]

What's your name?
Siapa nama Anda?
[siapa nama anda?]

What's his name?
Siapa namanya?
[siapa namanja?]

What's her name?
Siapa namanya?
[siapa namanja?]

What's your last name?
Siapa nama belakang Anda?
[siapa nama belakaŋ anda?]

You can call me …
Panggil saya …
[paŋgil saja …]

Where are you from?
Dari mana asal Anda?
[dari mana asal anda?]

I'm from …
Saya dari …
[saja dari …]

What do you do for a living?
Apa pekerjaan Anda?
[apa pekerdʒ'a'an anda?]

Who is this?
Siapa ini?
[siapa ini?]

Who is he?
Siapa dia?
[siapa dia?]

Who is she?
Siapa dia?
[siapa dia?]

Who are they?
Siapa mereka?
[siapa mereka?]

This is …	**Ini …** [ini …]
my friend (masc.)	**teman saya** [teman saja]
my friend (fem.)	**teman saya** [teman saja]
my husband	**suami saya** [suami saja]
my wife	**istri saya** [istri saja]
my father	**ayah saya** [ajah saja]
my mother	**ibu saya** [ibu saja]
my brother	**saudara laki-laki saya** [saudara laki-laki saja]
my sister	**saudara perempuan saya** [saudara perempuan saja]
my son	**anak laki-laki saya** [ana' laki-laki saja]
my daughter	**anak perempuan saya** [ana' perempuan saja]
This is our son.	**Ini anak laki-laki kami.** [ini ana' laki-laki kami]
This is our daughter.	**Ini anak perempuan kami.** [ini ana' perempuan kami]
These are my children.	**Ini anak-anak saya.** [ini ana'-ana' saja]
These are our children.	**Ini anak-anak kami.** [ini ana'-ana' kami]

Farewells

Good bye!	**Selamat tinggal!** [selamat tiŋgal!]
Bye! (inform.)	**Dadah!** [dadah!]
See you tomorrow.	**Sampai bertemu besok.** [sampaj bertemu beso']
See you soon.	**Sampai jumpa.** [sampaj dʒʲumpa]
See you at seven.	**Sampai jumpa pukul tujuh.** [sampaj dʒʲumpa pukul tudʒʲuh]
Have fun!	**Selamat bersenang-senang!** [selamat bersenaŋ-senaŋ!]
Talk to you later.	**Kita mengobrol lagi nanti.** [kita meŋobrol lagi nanti]
Have a nice weekend.	**Selamat berakhir pekan.** [selamat berahir pekan]
Good night.	**Selamat malam.** [selamat malam]
It's time for me to go.	**Sudah waktunya saya pamit.** [sudah waktunja saja pamit]
I have to go.	**Saya harus pergi.** [saja harus pergi]
I will be right back.	**Saya akan segera kembali.** [saja akan segera kembali]
It's late.	**Sudah larut.** [sudah larut]
I have to get up early.	**Saya harus bangun pagi.** [saja harus baŋun pagi]
I'm leaving tomorrow.	**Saya pergi besok.** [saja pergi beso']
We're leaving tomorrow.	**Kami pergi besok.** [kami pergi beso']
Have a nice trip!	**Semoga perjalanan Anda menyenangkan!** [semoga perdʒʲalanan anda menjenaŋkan!]
It was nice meeting you.	**Senang dapat berjumpa dengan Anda.** [senaŋ dapat berdʒʲumpa deŋan anda]

It was nice talking to you. **Senang dapat berbincang dengan Anda.**
[senaŋ dapat berbintʃaŋ deŋan anda]

Thanks for everything. **Terima kasih atas segalanya.**
[terima kasih atas segalanja]

I had a very good time. **Saya senang sekali hari ini.**
[saja senaŋ sekali hari ini]

We had a very good time. **Kami senang sekali hari ini.**
[kami senaŋ sekali hari ini]

It was really great. **Hari yang luar biasa.**
[hari jaŋ luar biasa]

I'm going to miss you. **Saya akan merindukan Anda.**
[saja akan merindukan anda]

We're going to miss you. **Kami akan merindukan Anda.**
[kami akan merindukan anda]

Good luck! **Semoga berhasil!**
[semoga berhasil!]

Say hi to … **Sampaikan salam saya untuk ...**
[sampajkan salam saja untu' ...]

Foreign language

I don't understand.	**Saya tidak mengerti.** [saja tida' meŋerti]
Write it down, please.	**Tolong tuliskan.** [toloŋ tuliskan]
Do you speak ...?	**Apa Anda bisa berbahasa ...?** [apa anda bisa berbahasa ...?]
I speak a little bit of ...	**Saya bisa sedikit berbahasa ...** [saja bisa sedikit berbahasa ...]
English	**Inggris** [iŋgris]
Turkish	**Turki** [turki]
Arabic	**Arab** [arab]
French	**Perancis** [perantʃis]
German	**Jerman** [dʒˈerman]
Italian	**Italia** [italia]
Spanish	**Spanyol** [spanjol]
Portuguese	**Portugis** [portugis]
Chinese	**Mandarin** [mandarin]
Japanese	**Jepang** [dʒˈepaŋ]
Can you repeat that, please.	**Bisakah Anda mengulanginya?** [bisakah anda meŋulaŋinja?]
I understand.	**Saya mengerti.** [saja meŋerti]
I don't understand.	**Saya tidak mengerti.** [saja tida' meŋerti]
Please speak more slowly.	**Tolong berbicara lebih lambat.** [toloŋ berbitʃara lebih lambat]
Is that correct? (Am I saying it right?)	**Apakah itu benar?** [apakah itu benar?]
What is this? (What does this mean?)	**Apa ini? (Apa artinya ini?)** [apa ini? (apa artinja ini?)]

Apologies

Excuse me, please.	**Permisi.** [permisi]
I'm sorry.	**Maaf.** [ma'af]
I'm really sorry.	**Saya benar-benar minta maaf.** [saja benar-benar minta ma'af]
Sorry, it's my fault.	**Maaf, itu kesalahan saya.** [ma'af, itu kesalahan saja]
My mistake.	**Saya yang salah.** [saja jaŋ salah]
May I ...?	**Boleh saya ...?** [boleh saja ...?]
Do you mind if I ...?	**Apakah Anda keberatan jika saya ...?** [apakah anda keberatan dʒika saja ...?]
It's OK.	**Tidak apa-apa.** [tida' apa-apa]
It's all right.	**Tidak apa-apa.** [tida' apa-apa]
Don't worry about it.	**Jangan khawatir.** [dʒ'aŋan hawatir]

Agreement

Yes.	**Ya.** [ja]
Yes, sure.	**Ya, tentu saja.** [ja, tentu sadʒʲa]
OK (Good!)	**Bagus!** [bagus!]
Very well.	**Baiklah.** [baiklah]
Certainly!	**Tentu saja.** [tentu sadʒʲa]
I agree.	**Saya setuju.** [saja setudʒʲu]

That's correct.	**Betul.** [betul]
That's right.	**Benar.** [benar]
You're right.	**Anda benar.** [anda benar]
I don't mind.	**Saya tidak keberatan.** [saja tidak keberatan]
Absolutely right.	**Benar sekali.** [benar sekali]

It's possible.	**Mungkin saja.** [muŋkin sadʒʲa]
That's a good idea.	**Ide bagus.** [ide bagus]
I can't say no.	**Saya tidak bisa menolaknya.** [saja tida' bisa menolaknja]
I'd be happy to.	**Dengan senang hati.** [deŋan senaŋ hati]
With pleasure.	**Dengan senang hati.** [deŋan senaŋ hati]

Refusal. Expressing doubt

No.
Tidak.
[tida']

Certainly not.
Tentu saja tidak.
[tentu sadʒ'a tida']

I don't agree.
Saya tidak setuju.
[saja tida' setudʒ'u]

I don't think so.
Saya rasa tidak begitu.
[saja rasa tida' begitu]

It's not true.
Tidak benar.
[tida' benar]

You are wrong.
Anda keliru.
[anda keliru]

I think you are wrong.
Saya rasa Anda keliru.
[saja rasa anda keliru]

I'm not sure.
Saya kurang yakin.
[saja kuraŋ jakin]

It's impossible.
Tidak mungkin.
[tida' muŋkin]

Nothing of the kind (sort)!
Itu mengada-ada!
[itu meŋada-ada!]

The exact opposite.
Justru kebalikannya.
[dʒ'ustru kebalikannja]

I'm against it.
Saya menentangnya.
[saja menentaŋnja]

I don't care.
Saya tidak peduli.
[saja tida' peduli]

I have no idea.
Saya tidak tahu.
[saja tida' tahu]

I doubt it.
Saya meragukannya.
[saja meragukannja]

Sorry, I can't.
Maaf, saya tidak bisa.
[ma'af, saja tida' bisa]

Sorry, I don't want to.
Maaf, saya tidak mau.
[ma'af, saja tida' mau]

Thank you, but I don't need this.
Maaf, saya tidak membutuhkannya.
[ma'af, saja tida' membutuhkannja]

It's getting late.
Sudah semakin larut.
[sudah semakin larut]

I have to get up early.

Saya harus bangun pagi.
[saja harus baŋun pagi]

I don't feel well.

Saya tidak enak badan.
[saja tida' enak badan]

Expressing gratitude

Thank you.
Terima kasih.
[terima kasih]

Thank you very much.
Terima kasih banyak.
[terima kasih banja']

I really appreciate it.
Saya sangat menghargainya.
[saja saŋat meŋhargainja]

I'm really grateful to you.
Saya sangat berterima kasih kepada Anda.
[saja saŋat berterima kasih kepada anda]

We are really grateful to you.
Kami sangat berterima kasih kepada Anda.
[kami saŋat berterima kasih kepada anda]

Thank you for your time.
Terima kasih atas waktu Anda.
[terima kasih atas waktu anda]

Thanks for everything.
Terima kasih atas segalanya.
[terima kasih atas segalanja]

Thank you for ...
Terima kasih atas ...
[terima kasih atas ...]

your help
bantuan Anda
[bantuan anda]

a nice time
saat yang menyenangkan ini
[sa'at jaŋ menjenaŋkan ini]

a wonderful meal
hidangan yang luar biasa ini
[hidaŋan jaŋ luar biasa ini]

a pleasant evening
malam yang menyenangkan ini
[malam jaŋ menjenaŋkan ini]

a wonderful day
hari yang luar biasa ini
[hari jaŋ luar biasa ini]

an amazing journey
perjalanan yang menakjubkan ini
[perdʒ'alanan jaŋ menakdʒ'ubkan ini]

Don't mention it.
Jangan sungkan.
[dʒ'aŋan suŋkan]

You are welcome.
Terima kasih kembali.
[terima kasih kembali]

Any time.
Sama-sama.
[sama-sama]

My pleasure.
Dengan senang hati.
[deŋan senaŋ hati]

Forget it.

Jangan sungkan.
[ʤˈaŋan suŋkan]

Don't worry about it.

Jangan khawatir.
[ʤˈaŋan hawatir]

Congratulations. Best wishes

Congratulations!	**Selamat!** [selamat!]
Happy birthday!	**Selamat ulang tahun!** [selamat ulaŋ tahun!]
Merry Christmas!	**Selamat Natal!** [selamat natal!]
Happy New Year!	**Selamat Tahun Baru!** [selamat tahun baru!]
Happy Easter!	**Selamat Paskah!** [selamat paskah!]
Happy Hanukkah!	**Selamat Hanukkah!** [selamat hanuʔkah!]
I'd like to propose a toast.	**Saya ingin bersulang.** [saja iŋin bersulaŋ]
Cheers!	**Bersulang!** [bersulaŋ!]
Let's drink to …!	**Mari bersulang demi ...!** [mari bersulaŋ demi ...!]
To our success!	**Demi keberhasilan kita!** [demi keberhasilan kita!]
To your success!	**Demi keberhasilan Anda!** [demi keberhasilan anda!]
Good luck!	**Semoga berhasil!** [semoga berhasil!]
Have a nice day!	**Semoga hari Anda menyenangkan!** [semoga hari anda menjenaŋkan!]
Have a good holiday!	**Selamat berlibur!** [selamat berlibur!]
Have a safe journey!	**Semoga perjalanan Anda menyenangkan!** [semoga perdʒalanan anda menjenaŋkan!]
I hope you get better soon!	**Semoga cepat sembuh!** [semoga tʃepat sembuh!]

Socializing

Why are you sad?	**Mengapa Anda sedih?**
	[meɲapa anda sedih?]
Smile! Cheer up!	**Tersenyumlah! Bersemangatlah!**
	[tersenjumlah! bersemaɲatlah!]
Are you free tonight?	**Apa Anda punya waktu malam ini?**
	[apa anda punja waktu malam ini?]

May I offer you a drink?	**Boleh saya ambilkan Anda minuman?**
	[boleh saja ambilkan anda minuman?]
Would you like to dance?	**Maukah Anda berdansa?**
	[maukah anda berdansa?]
Let's go to the movies.	**Mari kita ke bioskop.**
	[mari kita ke bioskop]

May I invite you to …?	**Boleh saya ajak Anda ke …?**
	[boleh saja adʒiaʔ anda ke …?]
a restaurant	**restoran**
	[restoran]
the movies	**bioskop**
	[bioskop]
the theater	**teater**
	[teater]
go for a walk	**jalan-jalan**
	[dʒialan-dʒialan]

At what time?	**Jam berapa?**
	[dʒiam berapa?]
tonight	**malam ini**
	[malam ini]
at six	**pada pukul enam**
	[pada pukul enam]
at seven	**pada pukul tujuh**
	[pada pukul tudʒiuh]
at eight	**pada pukul delapan**
	[pada pukul delapan]
at nine	**pada pukul sembilan**
	[pada pukul sembilan]

Do you like it here?	**Apa Anda suka di sini?**
	[apa anda suka di sini?]
Are you here with someone?	**Apa Anda di sini bersama orang lain?**
	[apa anda di sini bersama oraŋ lain?]
I'm with my friend.	**Saya bersama teman saya.**
	[saja bersama teman saja]

I'm with my friends.

Saya bersama teman-teman saya.
[saja bersama teman-teman saja]

No, I'm alone.

Tidak, saya sendirian.
[tida', saja sendirian]

Do you have a boyfriend?

Kamu punya pacar?
[kamu punja patʃar?]

I have a boyfriend.

Aku punya pacar.
[aku punja patʃar]

Do you have a girlfriend?

Kamu punya pacar?
[kamu punja patʃar?]

I have a girlfriend.

Aku punya pacar.
[aku punja patʃar]

Can I see you again?

Bolehkah aku menemuimu lagi?
[bolehkah aku menemuimu lagi?]

Can I call you?

Bolehkah aku meneleponmu?
[bolehkah aku meneleponmu?]

Call me. (Give me a call.)

Telepon aku.
[telepon aku]

What's your number?

Berapa nomor teleponmu?
[berapa nomor teleponmu?]

I miss you.

Aku merindukanmu.
[aku merindukanmu]

You have a beautiful name.

Nama Anda bagus.
[nama anda bagus]

I love you.

Aku mencintaimu.
[aku mentʃintajmu]

Will you marry me?

Maukah kau menikah denganku?
[maukah kau menikah deŋanku?]

You're kidding!

Anda bercanda!
[anda bertʃanda!]

I'm just kidding.

Saya hanya bercanda.
[saja hanja bertʃanda]

Are you serious?

Apa Anda serius?
[apa anda serius?]

I'm serious.

Saya serius.
[saja serius]

Really?!

Sungguh?!
[suŋguh?!]

It's unbelievable!

Tak bisa dipercaya!
[tak bisa dipertʃaja!]

I don't believe you.

Saya tidak percaya.
[saja tida' pertʃaja]

I can't.

Saya tidak bisa.
[saja tida' bisa]

I don't know.

Saya tidak tahu.
[saja tida' tahu]

I don't understand you.

Saya tidak mengerti sikap Anda.
[saja tida' meŋerti sikap anda]

Please go away.

Silakan pergi saja.
[silakan pergi sadʒ'a]

Leave me alone!

Tinggalkan saya sendiri!
[tiŋgalkan saja sendiri!]

I can't stand him.

Saya tidak tahan dengannya.
[saja tida' tahan deŋannja]

You are disgusting!

Anda menjijikkan!
[anda mendʒidʒi'kan!]

I'll call the police!

Saya akan telepon polisi!
[saja akan telepon polisi!]

Sharing impressions. Emotions

I like it.	**Saya menyukainya.** [saja menjukainja]
Very nice.	**Bagus sekali.** [bagus sekali]
That's great!	**Hebat!** [hebat!]
It's not bad.	**Lumayan.** [lumajan]
I don't like it.	**Saya tidak menyukainya.** [saja tida' menjukainja]
It's not good.	**Tidak bagus.** [tida' bagus]
It's bad.	**Jelek.** [dʒ'ele']
It's very bad.	**Jelek sekali.** [dʒ'ele' sekali]
It's disgusting.	**Menjijikkan.** [mendʒidʒi'kan]
I'm happy.	**Saya senang.** [saja senaŋ]
I'm content.	**Saya puas.** [saja puas]
I'm in love.	**Saya sedang jatuh cinta.** [saja sedaŋ dʒ'atuh tʃinta]
I'm calm.	**Saya tenang.** [saja tenaŋ]
I'm bored.	**Saya bosan.** [saja bosan]
I'm tired.	**Saya lelah.** [saja lelah]
I'm sad.	**Saya sedih.** [saja sedih]
I'm frightened.	**Saya takut.** [saja takut]
I'm angry.	**Saya marah.** [saja marah]
I'm worried.	**Saya khawatir.** [saja hawatir]
I'm nervous.	**Saya gugup.** [saja gugup]

I'm jealous. (envious)	**Saya cemburu.** [saja tʃemburu]
I'm surprised.	**Saya terkejut.** [saja terkedʒʲut]
I'm perplexed.	**Saya bingung.** [saja biŋuŋ]

Problems. Accidents

I've got a problem.	**Saya sedang kesulitan.**
	[saja sedaŋ kesulitan]
We've got a problem.	**Kami sedang kesulitan.**
	[kami sedaŋ kesulitan]
I'm lost.	**Saya tersesat.**
	[saja tersesat]
I missed the last bus (train).	**Saya tertinggal bus (kereta) terakhir.**
	[saja tertiŋgal bus (kereta) terahir]
I don't have any money left.	**Saya tidak punya uang lagi.**
	[saja tidak punja uaŋ lagi]

I've lost my …	**… saya hilang.**
	[… saja hilaŋ]
Someone stole my …	**… saya kecurian.**
	[… saja ketʃurian]
passport	**paspor**
	[paspor]
wallet	**dompet**
	[dompet]
papers	**dokumen**
	[dokumen]
ticket	**tiket**
	[tiket]

money	**uang**
	[uaŋ]
handbag	**tas**
	[tas]
camera	**kamera**
	[kamera]
laptop	**laptop**
	[laptop]
tablet computer	**komputer tablet**
	[komputer tablet]
mobile phone	**ponsel**
	[ponsel]

Help me!	**Tolong!**
	[toloŋ!]
What's happened?	**Ada apa?**
	[ada apa?]
fire	**kebakaran**
	[kebakaran]

shooting	**penembakan** [penembakan]
murder	**pembunuhan** [pembunuhan]
explosion	**ledakan** [ledakan]
fight	**perkelahian** [perkelahian]

Call the police!	**Telepon polisi!** [telepon polisi!]
Please hurry up!	**Cepat!** [tʃepat!]
I'm looking for the police station.	**Saya sedang mencari kantor polisi.** [saja sedaŋ mentʃari kantor polisi]
I need to make a call.	**Saya perlu menelepon.** [saja perlu menelepon]
May I use your phone?	**Bolehkah saya meminjam telepon Anda?** [bolehkah saja memindʒʲam telepon anda?]

I've been …	**Saya telah …** [saja telah …]
mugged	**ditodong** [ditodoŋ]
robbed	**dirampok** [dirampoʔ]
raped	**diperkosa** [diperkosa]
attacked (beaten up)	**diserang** [diseraŋ]

Are you all right?	**Anda tidak apa-apa?** [anda tidaʔ apa-apa?]
Did you see who it was?	**Apa Anda melihat pelakunya?** [apa anda melihat pelakunja?]
Would you be able to recognize the person?	**Bisakah Anda mengenali pelakunya?** [bisakah anda meŋenali pelakunja?]
Are you sure?	**Anda yakin?** [anda jakin?]

Please calm down.	**Tenanglah dulu.** [tenaŋlah dulu]
Take it easy!	**Tenangkan diri Anda!** [tenaŋkan diri anda!]
Don't worry!	**Jangan khawatir!** [dʒʲaŋan hawatir!]
Everything will be fine.	**Semuanya akan baik-baik saja.** [semuanja akan baiʔ-baiʔ sadʒʲa]
Everything's all right.	**Semuanya baik-baik saja.** [semuanja baiʔ-baiʔ sadʒʲa]

Come here, please.

Kemarilah.
[kemarilah]

I have some questions for you.

Saya ingin menanyakan beberapa pertanyaan.
[saja iŋin menanjakan beberapa pertanja'an]

Wait a moment, please.

Tunggulah sebentar.
[tuŋgulah sebentar]

Do you have any I.D.?

Apa Anda punya kartu pengenal?
[apa anda punja kartu peŋenal?]

Thanks. You can leave now.

Terima kasih. Anda boleh pergi sekarang.
[terima kasih. anda boleh pergi sekaraŋ]

Hands behind your head!

Tangan di belakang kepala!
[taŋan di belakaŋ kepala!]

You're under arrest!

Anda ditangkap!
[anda ditaŋkap!]

Health problems

Please help me.	**Tolong bantu saya.** [toloŋ bantu saja]
I don't feel well.	**Saya tidak enak badan.** [saja tida' ena' badan]
My husband doesn't feel well.	**Suami saya tidak enak badan.** [suami saja tida' ena' badan]
My son ...	**Anak laki-laki saya ...** [ana' laki-laki saja ...]
My father ...	**Ayah saya ...** [ajah saja ...]
My wife doesn't feel well.	**Istri saya tidak enak badan.** [istri saja tida' ena' badan]
My daughter ...	**Anak perempuan saya ...** [ana' perempuan saja ...]
My mother ...	**Ibu saya ...** [ibu saja ...]
I've got a ...	**Saya ...** [saja ...]
headache	**sakit kepala** [sakit kepala]
sore throat	**sakit tenggorokan** [sakit teŋgorokan]
stomach ache	**sakit perut** [sakit perut]
toothache	**sakit gigi** [sakit gigi]
I feel dizzy.	**Saya merasa pusing.** [saja merasa pusiŋ]
He has a fever.	**Dia demam.** [dia demam]
She has a fever.	**Dia demam.** [dia demam]
I can't breathe.	**Saya tak dapat bernapas.** [saja ta' dapat bernapas]
I'm short of breath.	**Saya sesak napas.** [saja sesa' napas]
I am asthmatic.	**Saya menderita asma.** [saja menderita asma]
I am diabetic.	**Saya menderita diabetes.** [saja menderita diabetes]

I can't sleep.	**Saya susah tidur.** [saja susah tidur]
food poisoning	**keracunan makanan** [keratʃunan makanan]

It hurts here.	**Sakitnya di sini.** [sakitnja di sini]
Help me!	**Tolong!** [toloŋ!]
I am here!	**Saya di sini!** [saja di sini!]
We are here!	**Kami di sini!** [kami di sini!]
Get me out of here!	**Keluarkan saya dari sini!** [keluarkan saja dari sini!]
I need a doctor.	**Saya perlu dokter.** [saja perlu dokter]
I can't move.	**Saya tak dapat bergerak.** [saja ta' dapat bergera']
I can't move my legs.	**Kaki saya tak dapat digerakkan.** [kaki saja ta' dapat digera'kan]

I have a wound.	**Saya terluka.** [saja terluka]
Is it serious?	**Apakah serius?** [apakah serius?]
My documents are in my pocket.	**Dokumen saya ada di saku.** [dokumen saja ada di saku]
Calm down!	**Tenanglah dulu!** [tenaŋlah dulu!]
May I use your phone?	**Bolehkah saya meminjam telepon Anda?** [bolehkah saja memindʒam telepon anda?]

Call an ambulance!	**Panggil ambulans!** [paŋgil ambulans!]
It's urgent!	**Ini mendesak!** [ini mendesa'!]
It's an emergency!	**Ini darurat!** [ini darurat!]
Please hurry up!	**Cepat!** [tʃepat!]
Would you please call a doctor?	**Maukah Anda memanggilkan dokter?** [maukah anda memaŋgilkan dokter?]
Where is the hospital?	**Di mana rumah sakitnya?** [di mana rumah sakitnja?]

How are you feeling?	**Bagaimana perasaan Anda?** [bagajmana perasa'an anda?]
Are you all right?	**Anda tidak apa-apa?** [anda tida' apa-apa?]

What's happened?	**Ada apa?** [ada apa?]
I feel better now.	**Saya merasa baikan sekarang.** [saja merasa baikan sekaraŋ]
It's OK.	**Tidak apa-apa.** [tida' apa-apa]
It's all right.	**Tidak apa-apa.** [tida' apa-apa]

At the pharmacy

pharmacy (drugstore)	**apotek** [apote']
24-hour pharmacy	**apotek 24 jam** [apote' dua puluh empat dʒam]
Where is the closest pharmacy?	**Di mana apotek terdekat?** [di mana apote' terdekat?]
Is it open now?	**Apa buka sekarang?** [apa buka sekaraŋ?]
At what time does it open?	**Pukup berapa buka?** [pukup berapa buka?]
At what time does it close?	**Pukul berapa tutup?** [pukul berapa tutup?]
Is it far?	**Apakah tempatnya jauh?** [apakah tempatnja dʒauh?]
Can I get there on foot?	**Bisakah saya berjalan kaki ke sana?** [bisakah saja berdʒalan kaki ke sana?]
Can you show me on the map?	**Bisakah Anda tunjukkan di peta?** [bisakah anda tundʒu'kan di peta'?]
Please give me something for ...	**Berikan saya obat untuk ...** [berikan saja obat untu' ...]
a headache	**sakit kepala** [sakit kepala]
a cough	**batuk** [batu']
a cold	**masuk angin** [masu' aŋin]
the flu	**flu** [flu]
a fever	**demam** [demam]
a stomach ache	**sakit perut** [sakit perut]
nausea	**mual** [mual]
diarrhea	**diare** [diare]
constipation	**sembelit** [sembelit]
pain in the back	**nyeri punggung** [njeri puŋguŋ]

chest pain	**nyeri dada** [njeri dada]
side stitch	**kram perut** [kram perut]
abdominal pain	**nyeri perut** [njeri perut]

pill	**pil** [pil]
ointment, cream	**salep, krim** [salep, krim]
syrup	**sirop** [sirop]
spray	**semprot** [semprot]
drops	**tetes** [tetes]

You need to go to the hospital.	**Anda perlu ke rumah sakit.** [anda perlu ke rumah sakit]
health insurance	**asuransi kesehatan** [asuransi kesehatan]
prescription	**resep** [resep]
insect repellant	**obat antinyamuk** [obat antinjamu']
Band Aid	**plester pembalut** [plester pembalut]

The bare minimum

Excuse me, ...	**Permisi, ...** [permisi, ...]
Hello.	**Halo.** [halo]
Thank you.	**Terima kasih.** [terima kasih]
Good bye.	**Selamat tinggal.** [slamat tiŋgal]
Yes.	**Ya.** [ja]
No.	**Tidak.** [tidaʔ]
I don't know.	**Saya tidak tahu.** [saja tidaʔ tahu]
Where? | Where to? | When?	**Di mana? | Ke mana? | Kapan?** [di mana? | ke mana? | kapan?]
I need ...	**Saya perlu ...** [saja perlu ...]
I want ...	**Saya ingin ...** [saja iŋin ...]
Do you have ...?	**Apa Anda punya ...?** [apa anda punja ...?]
Is there a ... here?	**Apa ada ... di sini?** [apa ada ... di sini?]
May I ...?	**Boleh saya ...?** [boleh saja ...?]
..., please (polite request)	**Tolong, ...** [toloŋ, ...]
I'm looking for ...	**Saya sedang mencari ...** [saja sedaŋ menʧari ...]
the restroom	**kamar kecil** [kamar keʧil]
an ATM	**ATM** [a-te-em]
a pharmacy (drugstore)	**apotek** [apoteʔ]
a hospital	**rumah sakit** [rumah sakit]
the police station	**kantor polisi** [kantor polisi]
the subway	**stasiun bawah tanah** [stasiun bawah tanah]

a taxi	**taksi** [taksi]
the train station	**stasiun kereta api** [stasiun kereta api]

My name is …	**Nama saya …** [nama saja …]
What's your name?	**Siapa nama Anda?** [siapa nama anda?]
Could you please help me?	**Bisakah Anda menolong saya?** [bisakah anda menoloŋ saja?]
I've got a problem.	**Saya sedang kesulitan.** [saja sedaŋ kesulitan]
I don't feel well.	**Saya tidak enak badan.** [saja tida' enak badan]
Call an ambulance!	**Panggil ambulans!** [paŋgil ambulans!]
May I make a call?	**Boleh saya menelepon?** [boleh saja menelepon?]

I'm sorry.	**Maaf.** [ma'af]
You're welcome.	**Terima kasih kembali.** [terima kasih kembali]

I, me	**Saya, aku** [saja, aku]
you (inform.)	**kamu, kau** [kamu, kau]
he	**dia, ia** [dia, ia]
she	**dia, ia** [dia, ia]
they (masc.)	**mereka** [mereka]
they (fem.)	**mereka** [mereka]
we	**kami** [kami]
you (pl)	**kalian** [kalian]
you (sg, form.)	**Anda** [anda]

ENTRANCE	**MASUK** [masu']
EXIT	**KELUAR** [keluar]
OUT OF ORDER	**TIDAK DAPAT DIGUNAKAN** [tida' dapat digunakan]
CLOSED	**TUTUP** [tutup]

OPEN

BUKA
[buka]

FOR WOMEN

UNTUK PEREMPUAN
[untu' perempuan]

FOR MEN

UNTUK LAKI-LAKI
[untu' laki-laki]

T&P BOOKS

MINI DICTIONARY

This section contains 250
useful words required for
everyday communication.
You will find the names of
months and days of the week
here. The dictionary also
contains topics such as colors,
measurements, family, and
more

T&P Books Publishing

DICTIONARY CONTENTS

T&P Books Publishing

time	waktu	[waktu]
hour	**jam**	[dʒam]
half an hour	**setengah jam**	[seteŋah dʒam]
minute	**menit**	[menit]
second	**detik**	[detiʔ]

today (adv)	**hari ini**	[hari ini]
tomorrow (adv)	**besok**	[besoʔ]
yesterday (adv)	**kemarin**	[kemarin]

Monday	**Hari Senin**	[hari senin]
Tuesday	**Hari Selasa**	[hari selasa]
Wednesday	**Hari Rabu**	[hari rabu]
Thursday	**Hari Kamis**	[hari kamis]
Friday	**Hari Jumat**	[hari dʒumat]
Saturday	**Hari Sabtu**	[hari sabtu]
Sunday	**Hari Minggu**	[hari miŋgu]

day	**hari**	[hari]
working day	**hari kerja**	[hari kerdʒa]
public holiday	**hari libur**	[hari libur]
weekend	**akhir pekan**	[ahir pekan]

week	**minggu**	[miŋgu]
last week (adv)	**minggu lalu**	[miŋgu lalu]
next week (adv)	**minggu berikutnya**	[miŋgu berikutnja]

in the morning	**pada pagi hari**	[pada pagi hari]
in the afternoon	**pada sore hari**	[pada sore hari]

in the evening	**waktu sore**	[waktu sore]
tonight (this evening)	**sore ini**	[sore ini]

at night	**pada malam hari**	[pada malam hari]
midnight	**tengah malam**	[teŋah malam]

January	**Januari**	[dʒanuari]
February	**Februari**	[februari]
March	**Maret**	[marɛt]
April	**April**	[april]
May	**Mei**	[mei]
June	**Juni**	[dʒuni]

July	**Juli**	[dʒuli]
August	**Augustus**	[augustus]

September	September	[september]
October	Oktober	[oktober]
November	November	[november]
December	Desember	[desember]

in spring	pada musim semi	[pada musim semi]
in summer	pada musim panas	[pada musim panas]
in fall	pada musim gugur	[pada musim gugur]
in winter	pada musim dingin	[pada musim diŋin]

month	bulan	[bulan]
season (summer, etc.)	musim	[musim]
year	tahun	[tahun]

2. Numbers. Numerals

0 zero	nol	[nol]
1 one	satu	[satu]
2 two	dua	[dʋa]
3 three	tiga	[tiga]
4 four	empat	[empat]

5 five	lima	[lima]
6 six	enam	[enam]
7 seven	tujuh	[tudʒʲuh]
8 eight	delapan	[delapan]
9 nine	sembilan	[sembilan]
10 ten	sepuluh	[sepuluh]

11 eleven	sebelas	[sebelas]
12 twelve	dua belas	[dua belas]
13 thirteen	tiga belas	[tiga belas]
14 fourteen	empat belas	[empat belas]
15 fifteen	lima belas	[lima belas]

16 sixteen	enam belas	[enam belas]
17 seventeen	tujuh belas	[tudʒʲuh belas]
18 eighteen	delapan belas	[delapan belas]
19 nineteen	sembilan belas	[sembilan belas]

20 twenty	dua puluh	[dua puluh]
30 thirty	tiga puluh	[tiga puluh]
40 forty	empat puluh	[empat puluh]
50 fifty	lima puluh	[lima puluh]

60 sixty	enam puluh	[enam puluh]
70 seventy	tujuh puluh	[tudʒʲuh puluh]
80 eighty	delapan puluh	[delapan puluh]
90 ninety	sembilan puluh	[sembilan puluh]
100 one hundred	seratus	[seratus]

200 two hundred	**dua ratus**	[dua ratus]
300 three hundred	**tiga ratus**	[tiga ratus]
400 four hundred	**empat ratus**	[empat ratus]
500 five hundred	**lima ratus**	[lima ratus]
600 six hundred	**enam ratus**	[enam ratus]
700 seven hundred	**tujuh ratus**	[tuʤ'uh ratus]
800 eight hundred	**delapan ratus**	[delapan ratus]
900 nine hundred	**sembilan ratus**	[sembilan ratus]
1000 one thousand	**seribu**	[seribu]
10000 ten thousand	**sepuluh ribu**	[sepuluh ribu]
one hundred thousand	**seratus ribu**	[seratus ribu]
million	**juta**	[ʤ'uta]
billion	**miliar**	[miliar]

3. Humans. Family

man (adult male)	**laki-laki, pria**	[laki-laki], [pria]
young man	**pemuda**	[pemuda]
woman	**perempuan, wanita**	[perempuan], [wanita]
girl (young woman)	**gadis**	[gadis]
old man	**lelaki tua**	[lelaki tua]
old woman	**perempuan tua**	[perempuan tua]
mother	**ibu**	[ibu]
father	**ayah**	[ajah]
son	**anak lelaki**	[anaʔ lelaki]
daughter	**anak perempuan**	[anaʔ perempuan]
brother	**saudara lelaki**	[saudara lelaki]
sister	**saudara perempuan**	[saudara perempuan]
parents	**orang tua**	[oraŋ tua]
child	**anak**	[anaʔ]
children	**anak-anak**	[anaʔ-anaʔ]
stepmother	**ibu tiri**	[ibu tiri]
stepfather	**ayah tiri**	[ajah tiri]
grandmother	**nenek**	[neneʔ]
grandfather	**kakek**	[kakeʔ]
grandson	**cucu laki-laki**	[ʧuʧu laki-laki]
granddaughter	**cucu perempuan**	[ʧuʧu perempuan]
grandchildren	**cucu**	[ʧuʧu]
uncle	**paman**	[paman]
aunt	**bibi**	[bibi]
nephew	**keponakan laki-laki**	[keponakan laki-laki]
niece	**keponakan perempuan**	[keponakan perempuan]
wife	**istri**	[istri]

husband	**suami**	[suami]
married (masc.)	**menikah, beristri**	[mənikah], [bəristri]
married (fem.)	**menikah, bersuami**	[mənikah], [bərsuami]
widow	**janda**	[dʒʲanda]
widower	**duda**	[duda]
name (first name)	**nama, nama depan**	[nama], [nama depan]
surname (last name)	**nama keluarga**	[nama keluarga]
relative	**kerabat**	[kerabat]
friend (masc.)	**sahabat**	[sahabat]
friendship	**persahabatan**	[pərsahabatan]
partner	**mitra**	[mitra]
superior (n)	**atasan**	[atasan]
colleague	**kolega**	[kolega]
neighbors	**para tetangga**	[para tetaŋga]

4. Human body

body	**tubuh**	[tubuh]
heart	**jantung**	[dʒʲantuŋ]
blood	**darah**	[darah]
brain	**otak**	[otaʔ]
bone	**tulang**	[tulaŋ]
spine (backbone)	**tulang belakang**	[tulaŋ belakaŋ]
rib	**tulang rusuk**	[tulaŋ rusuʔ]
lungs	**paru-paru**	[paru-paru]
skin	**kulit**	[kulit]
head	**kepala**	[kepala]
face	**wajah**	[wadʒʲah]
nose	**hidung**	[hiduŋ]
forehead	**dahi**	[dahi]
cheek	**pipi**	[pipi]
mouth	**mulut**	[mulut]
tongue	**lidah**	[lidah]
tooth	**gigi**	[gigi]
lips	**bibir**	[bibir]
chin	**dagu**	[dagu]
ear	**telinga**	[teliŋa]
neck	**leher**	[leher]
eye	**mata**	[mata]
pupil	**pupil, biji mata**	[pupil], [bidʒʲi mata]
eyebrow	**alis**	[alis]
eyelash	**bulu mata**	[bulu mata]
hair	**rambut**	[rambut]

hairstyle	**tatanan rambut**	[tatanan rambut]
mustache	**kumis**	[kumis]
beard	**janggut**	[dʒ'aŋgut]
to have (a beard, etc.)	**memelihara**	[memelihara]
bald (adj)	**botak, plontos**	[botak], [plontos]

hand	**tangan**	[taŋan]
arm	**lengan**	[leŋan]
finger	**jari**	[dʒ'ari]
nail	**kuku**	[kuku]
palm	**telapak**	[telapa']

shoulder	**bahu**	[bahu]
leg	**kaki**	[kaki]
knee	**lutut**	[lutut]
heel	**tumit**	[tumit]
back	**punggung**	[puŋguŋ]

5. Clothing. Personal accessories

clothes	**pakaian**	[pakajan]
coat (overcoat)	**mantel**	[mantel]
fur coat	**mantel bulu**	[mantel bulu]
jacket (e.g., leather ~)	**jaket**	[dʒ'aket]
raincoat (trenchcoat, etc.)	**jas hujan**	[dʒ'as hudʒ'an]

shirt (button shirt)	**kemeja**	[kemedʒ'a]
pants	**celana**	[ʧelana]
suit jacket	**jas**	[dʒ'as]
suit	**setelan**	[setelan]

dress (frock)	**gaun**	[gaun]
skirt	**rok**	[ro']
T-shirt	**baju kaus**	[badʒ'u kaus]
bathrobe	**jubah mandi**	[dʒ'ubah mandi]
pajamas	**piyama**	[piyama]
workwear	**pakaian kerja**	[pakajan kerdʒ'a]

underwear	**pakaian dalam**	[pakajan dalam]
socks	**kaus kaki**	[kaus kaki]
bra	**beha**	[beha]
pantyhose	**pantihos**	[pantihos]
stockings (thigh highs)	**kaus kaki panjang**	[kaus kaki pandʒ'aŋ]
bathing suit	**baju renang**	[badʒ'u renaŋ]

hat	**topi**	[topi]
footwear	**sepatu**	[sepatu]
boots (e.g., cowboy ~)	**sepatu lars**	[sepatu lars]
heel	**tumit**	[tumit]
shoestring	**tali sepatu**	[tali sepatu]

shoe polish	semir sepatu	[semir sepatu]
gloves	sarung tangan	[saruŋ taŋan]
mittens	sarung tangan	[saruŋ taŋan]
scarf (muffler)	selendang	[selendaŋ]
glasses (eyeglasses)	kacamata	[katʃamata]
umbrella	payung	[pajuŋ]

tie (necktie)	dasi	[dasi]
handkerchief	sapu tangan	[sapu taŋan]
comb	sisir	[sisir]
hairbrush	sikat rambut	[sikat rambut]

buckle	gesper	[gesper]
belt	sabuk	[sabuʔ]
purse	tas tangan	[tas taŋan]

6. House. Apartment

apartment	apartemen	[apartemen]
room	kamar	[kamar]
bedroom	kamar tidur	[kamar tidur]
dining room	ruang makan	[ruaŋ makan]

living room	ruang tamu	[ruaŋ tamu]
study (home office)	ruang kerja	[ruaŋ kerdʒia]
entry room	ruang depan	[ruaŋ depan]
bathroom (room with a bath or shower)	kamar mandi	[kamar mandi]
half bath	kamar kecil	[kamar ketʃil]

vacuum cleaner	pengisap debu	[peŋisap debu]
mop	kain pel	[kain pel]
dust cloth	lap	[lap]
short broom	sapu lidi	[sapu lidi]
dustpan	pengki	[peŋki]

furniture	mebel	[mebel]
table	meja	[medʒia]
chair	kursi	[kursi]
armchair	kursi malas	[kursi malas]

mirror	cermin	[tʃermin]
carpet	permadani	[permadani]
fireplace	perapian	[perapian]
drapes	gorden	[gorden]
table lamp	lampu meja	[lampu medʒia]
chandelier	lampu bercabang	[lampu bertʃabaŋ]

| kitchen | dapur | [dapur] |
| gas stove (range) | kompor gas | [kompor gas] |

| electric stove | **kompor listrik** | [kompor listri] |
| microwave oven | **microwave** | [majkrowav] |

refrigerator	**lemari es, kulkas**	[lemari es], [kulkas]
freezer	**lemari pembeku**	[lemari pembeku]
dishwasher	**mesin pencuci piring**	[mesin pentʃutʃi piriŋ]
faucet	**keran**	[keran]

meat grinder	**alat pelumat daging**	[alat pelumat dagiŋ]
juicer	**mesin sari buah**	[mesin sari buah]
toaster	**alat pemanggang roti**	[alat pemaŋgaŋ roti]
mixer	**pencampur**	[pentʃampur]

coffee machine	**mesin pembuat kopi**	[mesin pembuat kopi]
kettle	**cerek**	[tʃere]
teapot	**teko**	[teko]

TV set	**pesawat TV**	[pesawat ti-vi]
VCR (video recorder)	**video, VCR**	[vidio], [vi-si-er]
iron (e.g., steam ~)	**setrika**	[setrika]
telephone	**telepon**	[telepon]